NUTTAL ~~~~~ ~~~~~

Finding th

Birse Construction LTD
Humber Rd   Barton-on-Humber
S
      Humberside   DN18 5BW

_____

Tutts Building Group Ltd
  PO Box 323
        Peter Ho 937
Harrogate Rd
    Greengale Bradford
  W Yorkshire BD10 0RD

_____

Angeof
   Chamber of Confe·

the right job

Contents

Acknowledgements

Finding the Right Job could not have been written without the help of our many clients who have successfully put our theory of job searching into practice. Their experiences and ideas have contributed to every aspect of the book. They are too numerous to mention but they know who they are and our thanks and continued good wishes go to them.

Our colleagues in Corporate Management Development have encouraged us along the way and we are indebted to them for their contributions. Thanks must also go to the staff of BBC Books and to the individuals who have typed the many drafts of this book, especially Marie Cooper who produced the final version.

Last and certainly not least we would like to thank our respective partners and families for their encouragement, support and patience while this book was being conceived and written. Without them . . .

Anne Segall and William Grierson *March 1990*

Introduction

Seventy-five per cent of candidates do poorly in interviews and feel anxious about them *not* because they are unsuitable for the job but because they lack the necessary interview skills.

Recruiters say that unsuccessful candidates are the ones who drift into their offices without any apparent preparation and only the vaguest idea of what they are going to say!

The majority of job seekers have never seen a well-presented CV let alone written one.

To many job seekers the hidden job market remains hidden so they are never able to tap this rich source of job opportunities.

For those people who are not familiar with the process of changing jobs these are just a small sample of the hurdles which need to be overcome! *Finding the Right Job* has been written to help you overcome these and the many other problems which are associated with the whole spectrum of job change.

The book includes information on all aspects of the job search from writing your initial application form to making the right impression at interview. It provides a practical approach, explaining what action is necessary at each stage and helping you decide on the best way to find the job that is right for you.

Many successful job searchers say that changing their job was the best move they made and the job-searching period was a valuable opportunity to evaluate their careers and broaden their horizons. *Finding the Right Job* will show you how to devise your own job-search action plan and help you develop and maintain a positive attitude throughout your job search. By doing this you will soon discover that finding the right job isn't as elusive as you once thought.

1 Your job search

You are looking for a new job. Perhaps you are bored with your present one and want promotion, a salary increase or a new challenge with a different company. Maybe you are redundant or unemployed after a period of training, or have had a career break and now wish to return to full or part-time work. Whatever the reason, embarking on a successful job search is no easy matter. It takes a great deal of effort and hard work to achieve your goal, especially if you want to obtain *the right job* and not just any job.

The world of work has changed dramatically in recent years and will continue to do so in the future. So it will help if we begin by looking at the environment you will be job searching in.

Setting the scene

No one can live their life without being affected by social, economic and political events. So in contemplating your job search you must be aware of factors which will affect the opportunities open to you.

There are two main factors, operating at present, which will affect your choice of future employment.

1   There will be more jobs available in the new technology and service industries and less in the manufacturing sector.

2   By the end of the decade there will be a third fewer school-leavers and graduates available to take up employment.

Interpretation and effects

Fewer jobs will be available in the manufacturing sector, as the decade progresses, because of the arrival of new technology. As more and more companies take up automation and computerisation fewer employees are needed.

The move towards this new technology will grow during the 1990s and accelerate after 1992 when our European competitors will be able to market their ideas and products freely in the UK. However, as jobs move out of the manufacturing sector new jobs are created in the service or new technology sectors such as computer-aided design, banking, insurance, leisure industries, management consultancies and public relations.

Department of Employment statistics show that between 1961 and 1981, 3.3 million jobs were lost in manufacturing while 2.2 million jobs were created in the service sector. This continuing trend has obvious implications for your job search. If for example your skills are traditionally based you may wish to think about retraining. If you have been a manager or trainer with a large manufacturing company perhaps you will want to consider learning new skills and work for a smaller company or consultancy in the future.

Where previously companies used to promise careers for life and the security that went with it, there are now no such guarantees. A school-leaver today can expect to have between five and ten different jobs in their lifetime, interspersed with periods of unemployment or retraining. When looking at your job change, therefore, you should ensure your new job gives you additional experience, training and skills which you can take with you to a future employer. It's also important to look after your finances, investing wisely and taking out pension plans to protect against possible periods of unemployment or retraining.

The last twenty years have also seen a successful challenge by women to their traditional role. More and more women have sought the personal and financial rewards that are available in the work place and they are steadily taking an increasing share of the labour market. This is particularly important when looking at the demographic trend mentioned earlier. As fewer young people are available for work companies will try to fill their vacancies with women who have had career breaks to bring up young families. Enlightened employers are starting to offer financial help towards child care and workplace nurseries to encourage female staff back to work. When job searching you should check what facilities a company offers and what you may be able to negotiate for.

Work to live or live to work?

With these changes in work trends come changes in our social and leisure activities. Many UK companies now offer more flexible work patterns which recognise that many people can and do want to balance their life style more equally between work and home. Some service industry jobs give you the opportunity to work as a home-based consultant and schemes such as flexitime, job sharing and phased retirement are becoming more and more popular. Again, while job searching find out what a company is offering and what plans they are developing for their future working practices.

Types of work

If the future is going to hold periods of unemployment and retraining you will need to consider how to positively market your time away from work when attending a job interview. The answer to this problem is to forget the traditional concept of work. Instead divide your time into periods of PAID and UNPAID WORK.

Work

Paid

A job for which you are given an agreed salary. It may be a job that is intrinsically rewarding or one which you would not choose to do unless you needed the money.

Unpaid

An activity you enjoy or feel is useful, and which you do for no other reason than personal or social fulfilment. For example, acting as secretary to a residents' association, organising a local drama group, fund raising for a favourite charity. Unpaid work can also cover an activity you do not enjoy but are obliged to do by agreement or necessity. For example, gardening in your block of flats, or DIY in the home.

The skills you exhibit are equally valid whether they are used for paid or unpaid work. As long as you match your skills to those needed for the vacancy you will be able to market yourself successfully at an interview. This model also holds true for those who have taken a career break or have been unemployed for time.

Future trends

Finding the right job has never been simple and future trends indicate that this will continue to be the case. But however bad the employment situation appears don't be tempted to take just any job, or the first job you are offered, because you are worried about being unemployed. Taking a job that does not match your skills and interests will leave both you and your employer disillusioned and demotivated. Do your homework, undergo retraining if necessary, and prepare thoroughly to find the job that is right for you.

Beginning your job search

You may be job searching while in full-time employment or while unemployed or on a career break. Whichever is the case it is important to establish a routine as soon as you can and to stick to it.

If possible you should set aside a space at home where you can work from. Make sure you have a good supply of stationery and folders for copies of your CV, application forms and covering letters. The sooner you establish a routine the easier your job search will become. It will also give you a framework for the day if you are no longer at work. Your daily or weekend routine should include:

–   visiting the local library to look at the adverts in the national and local papers.

–   preparation for any interviews that may be coming up.

–   writing speculative letters and making applications.

Award yourself treats when you feel you have achieved something positive, for example completing and posting an application form. If you let yourself drift, you will soon become demotivated. Try not to let your worries destroy either family or social life and don't ignore leisure activities; they help keep you in a positive frame of mind for your job search.

It is equally necessary that your family and friends realise how important your job-searching routine is. Share your triumphs and failures with them but try if you can to choose moments when they feel able to listen fully. If you are unemployed or redundant you will probably be at home a great deal more, and you must respect other people's living and working routines. They may not be used to having you around. It's important, therefore, that you work out a joint plan to help with increased chores and still put real effort into your job search.

Action planning

You are now ready to embark on your job search.

Begin by listing on a large sheet of paper *all* your skills and abilities. In the left-hand column write details of your employment, education, training and leisure activities. Against each topic write answers to the following questions:

> What do I actually do in terms of paid and unpaid work?
>
> What responsibilities do I have?
>
> Who am I responsible to and for?

What do I enjoy doing the most and the least?

What abilities do I have?

What achievements have I had?

If you find this difficult to do alone, ask a supportive partner, friend or colleague to help you. It's surprising what they will include that, through false modesty, you will have missed! Check that you have included *everything*. The exercise will result in a data-bank of information about yourself. You will be able to draw on this to complete application forms, letters and your CV. It will also help you extract information about yourself relevant to individual vacancies.

What do you want?

When you have completed the above exercise you should have a better idea of the skills, qualifications and experience you can offer a potential employer. You now need to analyse the sort of job you want.

You should consider:

(a) Job content
    think of the functions you know well and
    the tasks you are experienced in
    carrying out.

(b) Status

what level of responsibility are you looking for? Do you want a job that will lead to a future senior management position or simply increased job satisfaction? Which is more important, financial reward or job fulfilment?

(c) Salary

what is the minimum you need to keep up important or essential aspects of your life style?

(d) Location

discuss with, and consider the needs of, members of your family who will be directly affected by any decision you might make on moving home.

(3) Prospects

how ambitious are you? How hard are you prepared to work at furthering your career? For example, are you the sort of person who would move home if you were offered a promotion or work long hours at the expense of your family and social life?

It is important to be realistic about your prospects and the length of time it can take to find a new job. You may have to make many applications before you get an interview or job offer. But whilst being realistic and frank with yourself about any weak points, make sure you also recognise every possible asset you can offer a prospective employer.

Often something which at first sight looks like a weakness can in fact be a strength. Remember, age means experience and can be a strong selling point to the right employer. And while doing a specialised job for a long time with the same company may not be a recommendation to an employer looking for broad experience, to an employer in your own field, your background may be worth its weight in gold.

Remember you are entering a *job market* where you will have to *sell* yourself. Your strengths, experience, skills and achievements are your *selling point*.

Sources of job vacancies

By now you will have considered your own abilities and the type of job you would like. The time has now come to look for vacancies.

1   You should answer advertisements in the national, local or specialised press and also consider placing your own advertisement. Newspapers are available at your local library.

When you see the advertisement which describes just the job you are looking for, resist the temptation to send a photocopy of your CV under cover of a letter which adds very little to the information offered. Your aim should be to make inclusion in the shortlist for interview a likely event. This can be done if you proceed as follows.

Carefully read the information in the advertisement regarding:

Conditions of employment	Personal attributes
	Experience required
Type of candidate sought	Job specifications
Qualifications	Interests
Special skills	

and list what you consider to be the employer's main needs.

Write your covering letter highlighting those needs, saying briefly how you satisfy them and drawing attention to that part of your CV which provides the supporting evidence. CVs and covering letters are considered in detail in Chapters 2 and 3.

If the company asks you to complete an application form phrase the information you give in accordance with the wording in the original advert. Again include a covering letter and remember to keep a copy for future reference.

2   Send your CV to personnel recruitment agencies listed in *The Year Book of Recruitment and Employment Services* (available from your local library). They will look for suitable openings on your behalf if they feel

they have a good chance of placing you.

3   Call on any suitable local employment agencies.

4   Approach any professional organisation to which you belong.

5   See whether your present work contacts can make any introductions on your behalf.

6   Ensure that all your friends, acquaint-ances and contacts (both private and business) know you are looking for a job. If they cannot employ you directly they may know of suitable openings.

7   Identify potential employers who have not advertised and write them a speculative letter. Ask if they will see you for a general interview to discuss their company and future vacancies. Marketing yourself in this way keeps you ahead of the competition. The approach also gives you the initiative, as you decide which organisations, sectors, jobs and areas most interest you. Speculative approaches are dealt with in detail in Chapter 5.

Your next task is to compile a professional and well-presented CV.

2 Curriculum vitae and application forms

A curriculum vitae (CV), often referred to as a personal history form or career résumé, is the accepted, professional way of presenting your personal details on paper to an employer. Its purpose is to ensure that they quickly identify you as a potential candidate for a vacant position and so add your name to the list of people they wish to interview.

Your CV has to do a very important job on your behalf and so it's vital that you make it as positive and attractive as you possibly can. It should be brief (if it's longer than two sides of A4 the recruiter may not take the trouble to read through it), accurate and well thought out. It must also clearly list your strengths and achievements, showing what you have done and how well you have done it.

Your CV

Some sources say that you should write a new CV for each job you apply for. This gives you the opportunity to angle your previous experience to the vacancy on offer. If you have the time and resources this is a good idea, providing, of course, that you remember which version of your CV you have sent to which employer! However, few people have the capacity to produce several documents at once and if you are applying for two or three jobs each week you need to think seriously about the time and effort needed to complete several versions of your CV. A well-planned CV should take you 1–2 days to write and type up and it may be impractical to finish it in time to meet an advertised closing date, especially if someone else is typing it for you.

The solution to this problem is to have one standard CV which covers your career history in a general but positive way and then to include a *covering letter* with each CV, which states why you are specifically suited for the vacancy on offer. Covering letters are dealt with later in this chapter and in more detail in Chapter 3.

Layout
The following examples show you two alternative CV layouts. Which one you adopt is a matter of personal choice but however you decide to lay out your document do ensure that it is clearly typed and well presented.

Example 1

CURRICULUM VITAE

<u>NAME</u>   :

<u>ADDRESS</u>   :

<u>TELEPHONE NO.</u> : DAY:

                     EVENING:

(if you wish, include)
<u>DATE OF BIRTH</u> :   AGE:

<u>EMPLOYMENT DETAILS:</u>

(start with current or last job and work back)

<u>DATE</u>   COMPANY ADDRESS

<u>POSITION</u>   (e.g. Salesman, Engineer,
                           Warehouse Manager, Senior
                           Accounts Supervisor)

<u>DUTIES</u>

<u>DATE</u>   COMPANY ADDRESS

<u>POSITION</u>

DUTIES

*(continue as above and work back to your first job, giving more
generalised details of your duties each time)*

EDUCATION

DATE   SENIOR SCHOOL

DATE   COLLEGE/UNIVERSITY
                       (if applicable)

QUALIFICATIONS

OTHER TRAINING

INTERESTS AND HOBBIES

ADDITIONAL INFORMATION

e.g.
Available for immediate interview.
Date of birth and age *(if not included on first page)*.
Full driving licence.
Willing to work in UK and abroad.
Willing to relocate.

Example 2

Curriculum Vitae

CENTRE YOUR <u>NAME</u>

Give a brief summary (5 lines maximum) of who you are and the
position you require. For example:

I am a Careers Consultant working for a
large Media Company. I have experience of
counselling, training and producing careers
literature. I am looking for a management
position which will build on my experience
and develop my training role.

Address

Telephone no.   Day   Evening

Age (if you wish to include it here)

Present (or last) Employment Position

(CENTRE) Job Title and Company Address

Give details of your work.

(CENTRE) Qualifications and Training

Give details of the qualifications you obtained and training you received while holding this position.

(CENTRE) previous Job Title and Company Address

Give details of your work.

(CENTRE) Qualifications and Training

Give details as above.

Continue as above and work back to your first job, giving more generalised details of your duties and training each time.

(CENTRE TITLE) Education

(CENTRE) University/College Name
Date and Address

Details of qualifications obtained and grades.

(CENTRE) Senior School Name
Date and Address

Details of qualifications obtained and grades.

(CENTRE TITLE) Interests and Hobbies —

(CENTRE TITLE) Additional Information

Details as Example 1.

Having decided on your layout think carefully about which titles you want to emphasise and which details can go in lower-case letters. Use the full range of capitals, lower-case letters, underlinings and emboldened type to make your CV look as attractive as possible. Don't be tempted to overdo it however!

Too many emboldened titles or versions of typeface will make the document harder to read and will, therefore, distract the recruiter. The rule is to keep your CV clear and simple.

Compilation

You are now ready to consider the information that needs to be included on your CV.

Write down the points of information required in each category, making sure you have the correct dates, job titles and addresses to hand. Next, develop details of your employment history in an effective and positive way, avoiding jargon and abbreviations used by your present or previous employer which will mean nothing to recruiters in other organisations.

The data from the Action Plan you completed in Chapter 1 will also help you to give clear and precise details of your position and duties, while showing a potential employer the skills you have and how you have been successful. Remember, if a potential employer reads of your success in your previous job they are going to want to interview you to see if you can bring the same success to their company.

You should make use of the action verbs listed below to illustrate your strengths, as these will give the recruiter a positive picture of you. But do take care to use them selectively: you don't want to sound too good to be true!

Action verbs

accomplished
approved
assisted
authorised
budgeted
compiled
completed
composed
conceived
consulted
controlled
dealt with
delivered
demonstrated
designed
developed
established
estimated
expanded
explained
finalised
guided
implemented
initialled
instructed
introduced
learned
managed
motivated
negotiated
organised
participated
performed
planned
prepared
promoted
reorganised
researched
scheduled
set up
solved
strengthened
supervised
trained
utilised
wrote

Personal details

Enter your full name and preferred title, home address, telephone numbers (day and evening), age and date of birth. Some older applicants prefer to include their age and date of birth at the end of their CV under Additional Information. This ensures that the recruiter reads about an individual's positive attributes without having first seen their age; it is felt that this can help rule out the possibility of age discrimination. In the end this is very much a personal choice and as potential age barriers vary from industry to industry and from company to company, it is impossible to set any hard and fast rules. However, recruiters *do* become suspicious if age is not included on a CV, and this may stop them from inviting you for an interview.

If you feel there is a chance that your candidature will be prejudiced by your age, you should counter it by making personal contact with the company. While your application is being processed, write a good covering letter, speak to as many contacts as you can and try to arrange a visit to the company and informal chat with the recruiter before your interview. If handled positively this will dispel any doubts they may have had about your candidature. The same method can be adopted if you are returning to work after a career break or have been unemployed for a considerable length of time.

Employment details

Start with your current or last job and work back, giving dates of joining and leaving your past employers. You do not need to state salaries at this stage (unless specifically asked to do so) or say why you left one job for another.

Next, list the companies, and/or departments within companies, you have worked for, with relevant addresses. You mustn't leave gaps of time unaccounted for on your CV or recruiters will wonder what you were doing in the gaps!

If you've had a period of unemployment or a break from paid work you must still account for your time. Show that you had a career break or a break in employment from . . . to . . . and then in a few lines state the *positive* things you did during this time. For example:

1   From May 1987 to January 1988 I had a career break during which time I learnt word processing and acted as General Secretary for a local charity group. This has improved my skills as an organiser and administrator.

If you are unable to write positively about additional activities during your period of unemployment you could adopt the following example:

2   From May to December 1988 *(insert additional periods of unemployment)* I had an employment break. During this time I was continually job searching with the aim of securing a promotional position/a career change/increased responsibility. I achieved this with *(insert name of company)* in *(month, year)*.

Position and duties
Write two or three short paragraphs to demonstrate your experience and skills. Identify clearly areas of responsibility. Be precise and positive and highlight any major successes and achievements.

Education
Colleges/universities: List colleges/universities you attended, with relevant dates.

Senior schools: List the schools you attended, with relevant dates.

Qualifications: State qualifications from schools, colleges/universities: examinations taken, grades obtained.

Other training: Put down all relevant courses, especially those that market you as an individual i.e., management courses, office administration skills, anything specialised like computers, photography, languages or training involving technical aptitude.

Interests and hobbies
Insert at least three topics to demonstrate leisure activities, for example sports, musical instrument played, voluntary work for a charity etc., membership of clubs or associations, DIY.

If the job you want relies on experience gained from your interests and hobbies rather than your work experience, you may wish to move this section to the front of your CV. For example, your interests are in the field of sport and leisure and you wish to become a sports instructor, but at present work as a computer operator. In this case refer to your sporting interests and achievements immediately after your personal details and before you go into the section on employment details and positions held.

Additional information
As shown in the example CVs, you may wish to add information here which does not fit into other categories.

Drafting
Once you have compiled the necessary information, type or write your CV in draft form and ask yourself the following questions:

1 Does my CV fit on to two pages of A4-sized paper?

2 Is is neat, tidy and well laid out with no spelling errors? Remember, faced with a mountain of applications employers often jump on wrong spelling and bad grammar as an excuse for rejecting people.

3 Are the names, dates, addresses and telephone numbers correct?

4 Does my employment history description, or interests and hobbies, do me justice in a positive and concise way?

5 Does my CV tell a potential employer in less than half a minute what my last job was and what I have done in the past?

6 Am I sure that I have not omitted anything important?

7 Have I used terms and words that will be understood by others?

8 Do I feel confident showing my CV to a friend or colleague for approval?

9 Does it tell a prospective employer that I am worth seeing for an interview?

10 Does my CV properly market me?

If the answer to all ten questions is yes and you are completely satisfied, have the final document carefully and attractively laid out and typed. Proof-read it thoroughly, then make a number of photocopies for future use.

You should keep your CV up to date. A regular review will ensure that you incorporate new experience or training relevant to your career. Even if your job application is successful, you never know when you may need to apply for another position.

The covering letter – first thoughts

Always include a covering letter with your CV, otherwise there may be little or no indication of what job you're after! It is unrealistic to forward a CV in the hope that a potential employer will try to match your skills to their needs. They don't have the time to do this so you must do the work for them.

The letter should serve as your introduction and give the reason why you are sending your CV, either in response to an advertised vacancy or as a speculative enquiry. Your CV has probably been structured to be directed at a wide range of employers so the letter is your chance to be specific and highlight any particular attributes you feel you have for the job for which you have applied.

The letter should be as brief as possible – three short paragraphs at most.

1   It should state why you are writing, what position you are interested in, the reference number if applicable and where you saw the vacancy advertised.
    The organisation may be advertising more than one vacancy, or, if you are writing speculatively, the company will need to know the type of vacancy you are looking for.

2   It should then draw the recruiter's attention to your CV and highlight one or two reasons why you are suitable for the job (i.e. 'You will see from my CV that I have X years' experience in . . .').

3   End the letter simply by stating that you look forward to hearing from the company in due course. There is little to be gained at this stage from waxing lyrical about the company and its product. The longer the letter the less chance it has of being read!

4   Read the letter through before sending it. If you *must* continue on to a second sheet ensure that the last line on the first page does not leave a negative impression. For example:

    '. . . although I have no *(over page)*

shortcomings'.

The rule is always to draft your letter before typing or writing the final version. Covering letters are dealt with in more detail in Chapter 3.

Application forms

Irrespective of how effective employers find your CV you will often be requested to complete an application form.

Follow carefully the instructions for application given in the advertisement. If they ask you to 'telephone for a job description and application form', do just that: do not respond by sending a copy of your CV. If you want to get that all-important interview you must take as much time and care with this form as you have in compiling your CV.

Organisations use application forms because it is easier for them to make comparisons, and it ensures they have all the information they require, which is sometimes omitted from CVs! The rules of presentation and compilation are, however, the same as for CVs.

1   The first thing to do on receiving an application form is to read it through carefully from beginning to end. Make

sure you have a copy of your CV beside you and use the information on your CV to help you complete the application form. Follow the instructions carefully, place the requested information in the correct boxes and make sure your dates, spelling and grammar are correct.

2   If you are able to photocopy the form, this can be useful for drafting answers; if not, draft your answers on a separate sheet of paper.

3   Some of the sections of the form will require straightforward, brief and factual answers. Others will require a more detailed response. For example 'What duties did you perform in your last job?' Draft and redraft the detailed answers before completing the final version and if possible angle your answers to key words in the job advertisement. So, for example, if the advert requires 'Good communication and organisational skills', in your answer you should include the information 'My last job used my organisational and communication skills to the full as I was responsible for the general office routine'.

4   Never leave gaps on the form or cram your answers into too small a space. Presentation is all important. If there is

not enough room for your answers,
attach another sheet, typed if possible.

5   Certain sections of the application, like
'Any Other Information' are the
opportunity for you to sell your skills,
effectiveness and achievements.

6   When you are completely satisfied that
you have completed the draft to the best
of your ability, write or type out the final
version, as requested, checking and
rechecking for errors! It is often helpful
to have a second person look over your
draft answers and the final form.

7   Return the form promptly, by the date
requested, and don't forget to keep a
copy! This will help you if you are
invited for an interview and will save
time when completing other applications.

8   Always include a covering letter with
your application form. This gives a
further opportunity to set your job
application apart from other contenders.

Finally

Make sure you keep copies of your CV or
application form and covering letters so you
have a quick reference point when you receive
a reply from the company. If you do not hear

immediately, don't despair. The company has probably had many replies to its advert and is taking time to sort through them. If, however, you have not heard after a fortnight it is acceptable to make a *polite* phone call to the company to ensure that they received your application. And remember, if you are sending your CV or application form and covering letter in reply to an advertised vacancy make sure you send them off in good time to meet the closing date. If no closing date is given, ensure that your application arrives within ten working days.

3 Covering letters

It doesn't matter why you are writing to a company, the rule is always the same; you must carefully prepare your letters to give a good impression of you. Even the letter you write to request an application form must be tidy and well structured. Remember, everything to do with your job application will be put on file and be available at the interview, so a terse note on rough or flowery notepaper simply will not do. It is stupid to prejudice your chances by adopting a sloppy approach. Right from the outset match your letters to the high standard of your CV and application forms and give the recipient of your letter the impression they are dealing with a confident and professional individual.

Your letters should be clearly addressed to the company or organisation concerned. Your address, the date and the name and address of the company should all appear at the top of the page, together with a reference number if you've been asked to quote one. Whenever possible write to a named individual, as this immediately personalises your application:

you are dealing with an individual like yourself, not an entire multinational corporation!
If you are writing speculatively the best course
of action is to phone through to the company's
reception and ask for the name of someone in
personnel. It is very rare for this simple
request to be refused, but if it is, write to:

> The Recruitment Manager
> Name of Firm

and begin your letter 'Dear Sir/Madam'. In this
case you should end your letter 'Yours faith-
fully'. If you are writing to a named individual
then you should end your letter 'Yours
sincerely'. Use your normal signature and
print or type your name underneath, adding
Mr, Mrs, Miss or Ms in brackets: this avoids
any confusion or irritation on the part of the
recipient, who may not be able to decipher
your signature!

Use plain writing paper. Some people are
prejudiced against lined, coloured, flowery or
scented paper; certainly never use scrap
paper. This is an occasion when you will gain
the advantage by being conventional.

The written application is the first obstacle
you have to negotiate in getting a job, so if you
want the job you must make your application
as attractive and clear as you possibly can. It
would be a great shame to be turned down
because of the tone or layout of your letter,
before an employer has had a chance to hear

what you have to say in support of your application at an interview.

The write approach

Ideally you should have your letters typed, but if this is not possible make sure you write clearly and legibly. The rule is always to draft your letter before typing or writing the final version. You can then be sure you have given the information required and that you have really done yourself justice in terms of your experience, qualifications and abilities.

It is very tempting to compile an all-purpose letter and send it out to all companies on all occasions. This is the lazy approach and should be avoided! While it is acceptable to have a standard letter asking for an application form (although you must remember to change the reference number each time) or for your speculative approaches, it is *not* permissible when you are writing in reply to a specific, advertised vacancy. If a prospective employer has asked for a letter in support of your application it must be tailored to that organisation. Your aim is to appear as attractive a candidate as possible: remember, the company is likely to receive a number of applications so from the outset you are competing with other candidates whose qualifications may be as good or better than your own. Your abilities, experience and achievements, as outlined in your CV, must be highlighted to match the experience the company is looking for. You must emphasise in your letter those points which make you a particularly good applicant. To do this you must *sell* yourself in a specific way and underline the special contribution you think you can make to the company. Find out what you can about the organisation from the advertisement or the company's own careers literature and then show in your letter that you are keen enough to have found out something about them.

As with your CV, avoid using jargon and abbreviations. You and your present company understand them – but will anybody else?

Unless the employer asks you for a detailed letter saying why you think your training and background are relevant, keep your letter short and to the point. Remember that whatever you write is likely to form the basis for questions when you get to the interview stage, so don't waffle and pad the letter with impressive-sounding generalisations that you won't be able to back up when you come to be questioned about them! The rule is to be specific. So for example, if the company has asked for computer experience, in your letter write 'I have had experience of the following computer software . . . . and can program in . . . .'.

If you can write a letter or indeed fill in a

form showing a link between something you have actually done and the job you are applying for the interviewer will have something concrete to question you about, giving you a further opportunity for showing just how suitable a candidate you are. What is more important is that you will be able to make a favourable impression because you will have led the interviewer to talk to you about areas you feel confident in.

If you are writing speculatively this rule still applies. You must *sell* yourself on paper. Your relevant qualifications and experience together with a line or two explaining why you are interested in the company and its products and services will ensure that your letter is well received. You should state that you understand there may not be any immediate suitable vacancies but would be glad to be informed if there are. You can also ask the recruiter for an information meeting to obtain general advice; you may well get this. Even if there is no job available a discussion of this sort acts as an introduction and will help in future applications to that company.

On the following pages you will find examples of the types of letter you will be sending while you are job searching. These should be studied and then adapted to your own needs and circumstance.

Write on . . . !

Example 1 – Letter in response to an advertised vacancy enclosing an application form or your standard CV

Your name
Your address
Date

The company's name and address
(plus reference number if quoted
in the advertisement)

Dear (Name *as mentioned in the advert or Sir/Madam*)

Please find enclosed my CV/completed application form in response to your recent advert in the *Daily* XYZ of the (*date*) for a . . . . with your company.

You will see from my CV/application form that I have good . . . . skills and would be happy liaising with customers and staff at all levels. My experience in . . . . is also very relevant because I am trained in word processing/computing/management and leadership. I am also interested in . . . . which I feel would be an advantage for the post of . . . .

I am interested in ABC Company because . . . . and was very interested to

read of your plans to . . . . as this is an
area of particular interest to me.

I would very much like to be considered
for the post of . . . . and am available
to attend for interview at any time.

I look forward to hearing from you in
due course.
Yours sincerely/faithfully

YOUR SIGNATURE
Your name printed
Enc.

The first letters you write will either accom-
pany your returned application form/CV in
response to an advertised vacancy or will be
sent with your CV as a speculative approach.

Example 2 – Speculative letter to a company
asking if it has any vacancies

> Your name
> Your address
> Date

The company's name and address

Dear *(Named person or Sir/Madam)*
Please find enclosed my CV. You will
see from my CV that I have . . . . . years'
experience with the ABC Company and that

my career before this included working in/
for . . . . as a . . . .

I have a wide range of experience
including . . . .
. . . .
. . . . I am
also trained in/have experience of . . . .
. . . .
. . . .
. . . .

I have good communication skills, work
well on my own initiative and as a member
of a team and am a good administrator and
organiser/warehouse manager/retail
supervisor etc.

I now wish to broaden my career base
and wonder if you are anticipating any
suitable vacancies in the near future for
which I could be considered. I am extremely
interested in (name of company) because
. . . .
. . . . and find your plans to . . . .
. . . . interesting as I have
experience of . . . . I look
forward to hearing from you.
Yours sincerely/faithfully

YOUR SIGNATURE
Your name printed.
Enc.

If you are returning to work after a career break you could mention this in the last paragraph:

> For the last eighteen months I have had a career break during which time I . . . . I now wish to return to full-time/part-time work and wonder if you are anticipating any suitable vacancies in the near future for which I could be considered.

Your letter should then continue on as in Example 2 ('I am extremely interested in (*name of company*) . . .').

People often write speculatively to companies because they have seen them advertising other vacancies. If, for example, a company advertises for twenty-five computer operators, they may be expanding and will soon need supervisors and managers. The following letter covers this situation.

Example 3 – Speculative letter to a company that has recently advertised vacancies and which might require other categories of staff

Your name
Your address
Date

The company's name and address

Dear (Named person as mentioned in the advert.)

I was interested to see your recent advert in the Daily XYZ for a . . . .

I realise this means that . . . . Company Ltd is expanding and I am therefore writing to ask if you have any openings in . . . . which would suit someone with my qualifications and experience.

I am interested in developing my work in . . . . seeking wider opportunities in . . . . and wonder if your proposed expansion would bring forth openings in this area.

I have been employed as . . . . at . . . . for the past . . . . . years.

I enclose details of my background and of positions held. I have particular interests/ experience in . . . . which would appear

to be relevant to the work for which your
company is known. I am keen to develop the
work I have done at . . . . and think I
could make a useful contribution in your
own . . . . department.

   I understand that you may have no
immediate vacancies in this field; I should
however be grateful for any advice you can
offer me and hope that I may come and see
you or one of your staff.
With many thanks.
I look forward to hearing from you.
Yours sincerely/faithfully

YOUR SIGNATURE
Your name printed.
Enc.

The closing paragraph of Example letter 3
refers to the possibility of an informal interview with a member of the company. An interview of this kind, known as *an information
meeting*, has two functions:

1   It is an extremely good way of finding
    out more about a company and its
    forthcoming vacancies.

2   It gives you the opportunity to market
    yourself positively to a potential
    employer.

Although not widely known, it is in fact common practice for individuals to write to companies requesting information meetings.

Make sure you do your homework on the company before you go to such a meeting and *always* take a copy of your CV with you.

These meetings are dealt with in further detail in Chapter 5.

Example 4 – Letter requesting an information meeting

> Your name
> Your address
> Date

The company's name and address

Dear (*It is most important that you write to a named person when requesting an information meeting*)

Please find enclosed my CV. You will see from this I am working as a . . . . in the . . . . department of the ABC company. This has given me experience in . . . . and has established my skills as . . . . I am fully conversant with . . . . and have been trained in . . . .

I now wish to broaden my career base/

widen my opportunities in/develop my work
in the field of . . . . . .

Your name has been given to me by a
colleague/I saw your name in a recent
advert/directory/I was given your name by a
colleague of yours at a recent . . . .
conference. He/she suggested I write to you
to find out more about . . . . as I
believe you may well have the sort of
position I would be able to make a
contribution in.

Would it be possible to have a brief
meeting with you some time to discuss
. . . . Company Ltd and the types of
vacancy that might be suitable for someone
with my background?

I thank you for your attention and look
forward to hearing from you.
Yours sincerely

YOUR SIGNATURE
Your name printed.
Enc.

NB: Do not despair if you are not granted a
meeting. This is not a reflection on you; it is
simply that the individual is inundated with
similar requests. At the very least you will be
sent information which will help you with
your job search.

Example 5 – Thank-you letter after an information meeting

Your name
Your address
Date

The company's name and address

Dear (Named person)

I am writing to thank you for the very useful meeting of (date). It was very kind of you to take the time to see me.

I was particularly interested in the expansion of your . . . . department/ new training scheme for/new posts in . . . . and the possibility of future vacancies occurring for someone with my background and experience.

Thank you also for retaining my CV and forwarding it to the Personnel Department/ Computer Department.

I will now look out for the . . . . advertisements in the *Daily XYZ*/local newspaper/*ABC* magazine, as you suggested, and will make a formal application when I see a suitable vacancy.

Thank you once again for your time and trouble.

Yours sincerely

YOUR SIGNATURE
Your name printed.

The more *politely persistent* you are in your letter writing the more chance there is of making a good impression and securing the right job.

The ten golden rules of letter writing

You will need to write a wide range of letters during your job-searching period. The examples shown will act as a guide, but even if your needs are more specialised and specific you should always follow the *ten golden rules of letter writing*. This will ensure your letters are always written to an acceptable professional standard.

1 Keep your letters short and to the point: you should aim for three or four short paragraphs on one side of A5 or A4 paper.

2 Don't mention the salary you require in your letter unless specifically asked to do so. If you must mention it, always quote a salary range, not a specific figure. This will leave you room for future negotiation.

3 If a reference number was given in an advert make sure you quote it when you reply.

4   However much you want the job don't plead in your letter or sound too pushy.

5   Be polite and confident.

6   Keep your letters neat and tidy. Don't worry if they are not typed as long as they are clearly legible.

7   Ensure all your facts and dates are correct.

8   Make sure there are no spelling mistakes or wrong numbers – especially your telephone number.

9   Under your signature, print or write your full name.

10   Always, *always* keep a copy for future reference.

4 Interview success

Your contacts with potential employers will result in invitations to interview. At this stage the employer is seriously interested in you because your CV detailing your experience and achievements have made them feel you might well satisfy the job requirements. You, therefore, need to make a good impression at interview to give yourself the best possible chance of securing the job. Seventy-five per cent of candidates do poorly in interviews and feel anxious about them *not* because they are unsuitable for the job but because they lack the necessary interview skills. This chapter introduces these skills and helps you develop them. Once you begin to put them into practice you will find that interviews become stimulating and rewarding experiences which will lead you to *interview success* and a firm *job offer*.

First of all it is important to remind yourself of the purpose of the interview. It provides the employer with an opportunity to judge your suitability for the job and assess you in relation to other candidates. It is also your chance to find out more about the job and the organisation of the company you might be working for.

Pre-interview preparation

Researching the organisation

The first essential step towards a successful interview is preparation and if you are to succeed this must begin long before you enter the interview room. Recruiters are immediately put off by applicants who drift into their offices without any apparent preparation and only the vaguest idea of what they are going to say! The reason most people give a poor account of themselves is because they are nervous. These nerves are, in fact, a throwback to our cave-dwelling origins! In the face of danger or uncertainty our ancestors either fought or took flight, so symptoms such as increased breathing rate, sweating and pumping adrenalin to the limbs served them well. However, these classic signs of nerves are not at all useful for the twentieth-century recruitment interview! They make us freeze or become unnecessarily verbose, stumble over our words and appear clumsy and uncoordinated, traits which are guaranteed not to impress company recruiters. There are two ways to overcome these pre-interview nerves.

1 Make sure you prepare thoroughly before the interview. Research the company and its products, know the name of your interviewer and how to get to the company and above all think about the questions you'll be asked and work out effective answers to them.

2 It may sound obvious but try to *relax*. Once you know something about the company you won't be embarking on a journey into the unknown, so the element of 'fright' will begin to diminish. While you're waiting to go into the interview room take long slow breaths to control your breathing rate. Once this slows down, the other signs of nerves will begin to disappear and you will be able to greet the recruiter in a relaxed and positive manner.

No matter how many interviews you've had or how many you still have to attend you must be able to convince an interviewer that you are *genuinely* interested in working only for the company that is interviewing you.

Researching the organisation before you attend for interview will, therefore, benefit you in two ways:

1 You will be able to answer questions on the company and your potential role in it. This, in turn, will improve your

presentation and ensure you sound confident, organised and motivated.

2 The company will be impressed by the knowledge you display and the effort you have put into your interview preparation. If you can show them you have worked hard for the interview they will believe you will work hard for the company if they offer you the job.

Begin by building on some basic facts. Does the company manufacture products? If so, what kind of products does it produce, who does it sell to and where are its plants, offices or stores located? Or does this company provide a service, such as banking, retail or marketing? Where is its corporate head-quarters? How many branch offices does it have?

If the firm is a public company check the business pages of the national newspapers for information on it and the public library for a copy of its annual report. The best source of information though, is the company itself. When you are invited for interview ask the company to send copies of its sales and promotional brochures; it will be happy to do so and you will be showing tangible evidence of your interest. Additionally, if you have been sent for interview via an agency you will be able to get further information from your consultant.

The more you know about the company the more you can use this information to achieve the results you want.

Analysing the job specification/advert

Now you know about the company it's time to find out the qualities they want from the successful candidate.

Your first task is to read the job advert thoroughly and carefully. It's surprising how many people miss key facts about a job simply because they haven't studied the advert.

Take an A4 sheet of paper and write down the information from the advert regarding:

> *Conditions of employment*
>
> *Type of candidate sought*
>
> *Qualifications*
>
> *Specialist skills and experience*
>
> *Personal attributes and interests*

Add to this list any information you found from your research regarding the company's environment, product, staffing levels etc. You can now use this data bank as your own marketing tool. Write down how *you* meet the criteria asked for in the advert, especially any responsibilities you have had and general abilities which make you a particularly *good* candidate.

Some companies also issue job descriptions

and person specifications. These outline in detail the content and duties of the job and the qualities they expect from the person who will fill the vacancy. If you are not sent these you should phone the company to see if it can supply them. The job description and person specifications will give you useful additional information for your preparation.

You will definitely be asked questions at the interview on the criteria included in the advert and from the job description and person specifications, if you have them. Make sure you can explain how your experience, abilities, motivation and so on, meet the company's specifications and remember, the better prepared you are the more confident you will appear.

Building your image and identifying your qualities:

The marketing approach

An advertiser wouldn't dream of selling a product by saying 'This product is the same as all the others, there's nothing special about it and in fact in certain conditions it doesn't work at all!'

Yet it is amazing how many people go to interviews and say just that! They admit to failures and weaknesses, lack of experience and no real knowledge of the company they're hoping to join. They then become terribly demoralised when they don't get the job.

If the above approach is wrong for marketing products then it's definitely wrong for marketing *you*!

Build your image and your presentation style by concentrating before the interview on a well-thought-out marketing strategy. Begin with:

Product knowledge

Do you know yourself? Can you talk in detail about your achievements, qualities and skills? Do you know the key dates of projects you have undertaken and courses you have attended? Can you talk with confidence about experiences you have had and responsibilities you have been given? If you can't, write them down and practise talking about them. The more you practise the more confident and convincing you will sound.

Market research

Do you know your customer, that is, the company you are hoping to work for? Ask yourself: what does the company need and how can I provide it?

Packaging and display

Control your presentation during the interview. You need to project confidence and enthusiasm.

Speak clearly and concisely. Don't waffle away from the point and certainly don't give 'one word' answers: you'll make the recruiter work too hard and lose their interest.

Cultivate a firm handshake and look the interviewer in the eye while you are answering questions. Make sure you don't slouch or sit on the edge of your chair fidgeting nervously. Sit down, make yourself comfortable and look interested at all times.

Dress should be appropriate. Your aim is to look well groomed and professional. Don't try to look different; you want to come across as a reliable member of the team. If in doubt, go for a smarter version of how you'll dress for work. Remember, you want the interviewer to pay attention to you and the qualities you have to offer, so make sure your clothes enhance rather than distract from that message.

Advertising and promotion
Make sure that any contact you have with the company before your interview is polite and positive. Don't be rude to the receptionist or brusque on the phone. If you are writing to the company, ensure that your letter is well presented, and if you are looking round before the interview, concentrate on *public relations*. Be positive and interested in the information you are given and in what is happening around you.

Above all don't undervalue yourself.

Your unique selling point
You are unique. There is a quality about you that no other candidate for the job possesses. Focus on this quality (a position you have held, responsibility you have taken, etc.) and use it as your *unique selling point*.

This will make you stand out from the other candidates and ensure that the recruiter remembers you *apart* from the rest of the field.

Even if you have been away from paid employment for some time, either having a career break or because of unemployment, you still have a *unique selling point*. During your time away from paid work you may have learnt a new skill, for example word processing, computer operations, administration for voluntary groups. Or you may have taken up a new interest such as amateur dramatics, a foreign language or marriage guidance counselling. Any new skill or interest can provide you with your *unique selling point*. Remember, it doesn't have to be something you've been paid for or a complicated project, simply something you're good at that gives you confidence and makes the interviewer remember you.

Preparing for your interview
Know the exact place and time of your interview. Use a map and familiarise yourself with the location so you don't get lost. *A late arrival is never excusable.* At best you will only

antagonise the recruiter and make yourself anxious and nervous – certainly not the best way to begin the last phase of your job search!

Remember to bring a copy of your CV or application form with you, as the company may want to see it. They may also want you to fill in an extra form which you won't feel confident completing without the relevant information at your fingertips.

Know your interviewer's name, correct pronunciation and his/her title. Greet the interviewer by his/her surname and shake hands firmly. Remember, now is the time to begin your positive approach. Talk to the interviewer on the way into the interview room. Statements like 'your company was easy to find' or 'what nice modern offices' will ensure you begin to create a good impression. Don't overdo it though. Being over-friendly will not win you the job. If the secretary or receptionist greets you and shows you to the interview room, be polite; they may well be asked how you behaved. If you are kept waiting, receive any apologies gracefully and don't make a fuss, however angry and frustrated you may feel. This is not the time to antagonise the interviewer. Memorise the experience as a point of candidate care that you will improve if you join the company; this will help you keep calm and maintain your positive approach.

Before you go into the interview room you may be asked if you would like to leave your coat, bags etc. outside. *Do so.* Taking outdoor wear inside the interview room makes you look like an 'outsider' and you want to create the impression of already being on the 'inside' of the company. Similarly, don't refer to your present employer as 'we'. 'We do our accounts this way.' 'We've manufactured components like this for several years.' Speaking in this way again puts up a barrier between you and the recruiter. So whenever possible talk about your present employer in the third person. 'At ABC company I . . .'; 'The ABC company method is to . . .'.

Remember too that the interviewer may be nervous, indeed it could be their first interview as a recruiter! So help them (and yourself) as much as possible. Be polite and assertive, smile as much as you can and look them in the eye. This will help you create a positive impression and so help you relax. The more relaxed you are the more confident you will sound.

Written tests

It is possible that before or after the interview the company will want to give you a short test to provide evidence of the skills you talk about during the interview. Don't panic! You are not being singled out; all the candidates for the job will be asked to complete the same test. It may consist of short answers or ticking answer boxes in a multiple-choice questionnaire.

Whatever the form, follow the instructions carefully, work methodically through the test and leave yourself time to check your answers at the end. If you are faced with a particularly difficult question which you can't answer, leave it and go back to it if there's time at the end. It is better to do yourself justice by answering well those questions you know than by wasting time on those you do not. If you are applying for a clerical or secretarial job that asks for typing skills you can be sure the company will give you a typing test, so brush up your speeds and accuracy before you go!

In all cases the company will inform you beforehand, either by letter or at the start of the interview, whether they wish you to take a test and the form the test will take.

The interview

Some sources say that interviews are won or lost in the first 45 seconds. This may or may not be the case, but the message the statement carries is a clear one: *First impressions count and so you must get your interview nerves under control as soon as possible.* Your initial answers will sound more coherent if you have prepared a short résumé of your current position. Initial questions usually concentrate on 'what are you doing now' or 'tell us something about yourself'. The résumé will help you remember key points you want to make and enable you to highlight your achievements, skills and successes. These are your selling points and so need emphasising as often as possible.

Your task is to sound positive about yourself. Don't admit a weakness without showing the ability to make up for it or a willingness to learn how to change it. Similarly, don't talk about what you *can't* or *won't* do, but about how you see yourself working effectively in the new job. A recruiter is unlikely to take on someone who has listed 101 reasons that convey difficulty about working for their company.

Remember too that a successful interview is a *two-way* process. The employer is trying to determine if you have the necessary qualifications and experience for the job opening. You must determine whether the company will give you the opportunity to achieve your potential growth and development. You'll help this process work if you answer questions clearly and concisely and *listen carefully* to the information the recruiter gives you about the job.

Who will interview you?
No two firms interview in the same way. At one interview you may find your future manager and a representative from personnel, at another there may be up to five interviewers

from various interested departments. Don't panic or be put off by a sea of faces. You are not expected to take them all on at once! No matter how many people are present, in every case the rule remains the same. Each interviewer will ask you about a different aspect of your experience and the vacancy on offer. Once you have been introduced give your full attention and establish eye contact *only* with the person asking the questions. In this way you will maintain your confidence and concentration levels and ensure you give sufficient time and attention to each interviewer and the questions they ask.

Preliminary and subsequent interviews

You may find when you arrive for your interview that it takes the form of a preliminary discussion. At this stage one or two managers will interview you, asking you questions about your background and experience. On the strength of this they will judge your suitability to go forward for a second or final interview. Alternatively you may attend only one interview with up to five interviewers. The outcome will then depend on your performance at the time, compared with other applicants. The company will usually tell you what form this and subsequent interviews will take.

Questions the interviewer may ask you

It is impossible to forecast all the questions
you might be asked at an interview, but experience has shown that there are a number that
commonly arise. You should anticipate these
and work out appropriate and effective
answers to them. Look at the questions on the
next few pages and tailor them to your specific
purpose.

Introductory questions

> *Tell us something about yourself*

> *What is your present position?*

> *What project are you working on at the
> moment?*

These introductory questions are asked to help
you settle down while you talk about a subject
you know something about – namely you!
They are used by the recruiter to find out who
you are and what you do and it may also help
you to realise that they give the recruiter a
chance to relax and make sure they've col-
lected the right candidate!

Your aim should be to give the person interviewing you a well-explained and concise
résumé of yourself. Make three points (the
interviewer won't be able to absorb more); tell
them:

What you are doing now

The nature of your work

Briefly, what you did in your previous
position if you aren't currently in full-
time paid employment

This is more than enough information for the
recruiter to use to ask subsequent questions. It
will also act as a positive introduction to you
and will give some indication of the framework and structure you work within.

Don't be tempted to give too much information at this stage and remember, the recruiter
wants to know about you in a work context,
not about you and your domestic arrangements.

If you have been on a career break or unemployed for some time you need to think carefully about your answers to these introductory
questions. Try and pick up on the positive
things you've been doing since leaving paid
work. You may wish to focus on any new skills
and interests you've acquired or courses
you've taken. Above all sound positive about
your time away from paid work. You may wish
to include in your answer information about
your last paid job. It is up to you to decide
whether this is relevant or not and depends on
the length of time you have been away from
paid employment.

Career background

>Why are you leaving/did you leave your present/previous job?

>Why did you wait so long before thinking of moving from your present/previous job?

>Why have you not been able to find another job?

>Why did you take a career break?

>Why were you selected for redundancy?

>Wouldn't you rather work for a larger company?

>Would you find it difficult working for a commercial public company?

These questions will build up a picture of you and why you are seeking change.

Be positive when you talk about leaving your present or previous job. You are looking for a new challenge, promotion, increased training facilities, not more money. Also remember to emphasise that you are leaving a job or returning to work after a break, because you want *this* job with *this* company, not just any job.

If you have been in one job for some time emphasise the variety the job has given you and changes that have occurred, especially those you've instigated or implemented.

If you talk about redundancy, ensure you convey the impression that the post and/or department were made redundant and not you as an individual. Show that you have been looking for a position like the one the company is offering and are not prepared to take just any job.

Emphasis should also be put on the pressures you have worked under and the budgetary limits you have been able to meet. If you are moving from a large to a small company it may also be useful to say that the department you have worked for is medium-sized or small even though your company as a whole is vast. This gives the impression that you would have no trouble working with a smaller number of people in a close-knit team.

Personal attributes: your skills, achievements and strengths

> What do you see as your greatest strength as an employee?

> What have been your best achievements?

> What did you enjoy doing most in your last job?

> What are the qualities needed in a good secretary/clerk/administrative manager?

What do you feel you gained above all from your last job/your time away from paid employment?

If we offer you a job what are the greatest assets you have to offer us?

In what areas do you feel your expertise lies?

Here is your opportunity to shine! Make positive points about yourself drawn from your work and leisure experiences. If appropriate you can cite actual examples of how and where you've excelled. Your detailed preparation will help you here. You should also take the opportunity to make links between what you have done and the experience and qualities the company is looking for. So if, for example, in the advert the company mentions the ability to write reports and the recruiter asks the question at the interview 'What did you enjoy doing in your last job' make sure your answer includes reference to how much you enjoy report writing!

If you've never written a report at work but write them all the time for the local youth club or residents' association, then ensure you convey this information to the recruiter. Even though it's work you've undertaken in your leisure time it's still a skill the company is looking for. This is a simple technique to adopt and one that is very effective in practice.

Self-perception

> How would your present/past employer describe you?
>
> How would you describe yourself?
>
> How would your work colleagues/ friends describe you?
>
> What is your working/management style?

These, again, are questions which you need to answer by promoting yourself.

If you find it difficult to talk about your positive qualities in the first person then relate what other people (managers, friends or colleagues) have said about you. Here you should also think about the type of person the company has stated they are looking for and match your 'best' qualities to their person specification.

Your weaknesses

> What do you enjoy doing least at work?
>
> What things did you find most difficult in your last job?
>
> What areas would you feel least confident in if we offered you the job?
>
> What training do you feel you will need if you join us?

*How has your time away from work
affected you?*

*Why should we consider you with your
lack of experience in 'X'?*

*Do you feel your skills are too
specialised for us?*

The first thing to remember here is that
everyone has weaknesses and while you may
not have much experience of 'X' the other
candidates may know very little about 'Y',
your strongest attribute.

The rules for admitting a weakness are:

1 Ensure it's not a key requirement of the
job.

2 Immediately back up what action you are
taking/have taken to turn your weakness
into a strength. For example, you could
say 'My knowledge of French is rusty so
I'm taking an evening course to improve
it.'

If you are criticised for knowing too much or
too little about a subject balance the situation
by explaining what you do know, how other
named strengths you have will help you and
how you could help train others, given your
experience in a particular area.

These answers will impress recruiters as
they will see they have before them a

candidate who knows him or herself and can see *where* and *how* they can benefit the organisation.

Your temperament

> If people gossiped about you behind your back, what would they be saying?

> If faced with problem 'A' how would you handle it?

> Have you ever faced problem 'B'? How did you solve it?

> Are you a team member or a loner?

> Would working in a cramped office upset you?

> What makes you laugh?/What makes you angry?

These questions are asked in order to determine whether you'll fit into the company. Here again your preparation will help you. Be honest about yourself but don't be negative. 'I *won't* work in a cramped office' could just lose you the job. 'I'd rather not, but I'd make the most of it' will encourage the recruiter to see you as a positive person prepared to make the best of a bad situation.

Think what the company is looking for as you shape your answers – is it looking for a team player or someone to work alone? You should also ask yourself whether you will be happy with the arrangements the recruiter is telling you about.

Your research and perception of the job

How does this job fit in with your long-term career plans?

What do you think you'll be doing in three years' time?

Why do you think you are the best person for the job?

What can you contribute to this company?

Why should we offer you the job?

What did you do to prepare for this interview?

What do you know about this company?

How would your experience be put to best use here?

These are the key questions asked by recruiters to find out what you are going to offer the company and just how much you have tried to find out about them.

Concentrate on your *best qualities* when answering. Where appropriate – and especially if you find it difficult to talk positively about yourself – give examples of how your previous experience will be put to good use within the company. This is also the time to remind the recruiter of your *unique selling point* – you want to be remembered as a strong candidate with positive attributes to offer when the recruiter reviews this part of the interview. It is also important to give the recruiter the impression that you wish to stay with the company and take advantage of career and training opportunities. Unless a short-term contract is being offered, no recruiter is going to employ and spend money on training someone who they feel will only stay in the job for a short time.

Why do you want the job?

> *Why do you want to join this company?*

> *How do you feel you would fit in here?*

> *What important things do you look for in a job?*

It is surprising how many candidates cannot answer the question 'Why do you want this job?' Yet it is the one above all others that requires a well-thought-out answer. Tailor your answer to the criteria the company has given you and if the question is asked in the abstract, i.e. 'What is your ideal job?', make sure you answer by describing the job on offer!

Your arrangements

> How far will you have to travel daily if you join us?
>
> The company will be moving to 'X' next year, will this be a problem for you?
>
> How would you feel being away from home five nights a month?
>
> What were your earnings in your last job?
>
> Is the salary level important to you?
>
> Will your career break affect your future working arrangements?

When the recruiter begins to ask specific questions such as these you know you are coming to the end of the interview, but you must continue to present a positive image.

Use this opportunity to reassure the recruiter that travelling long distances, attending training programmes etc. present no problems to you.

Don't say 'No' I won't move, I won't travel etc. Wait until you are offered the job: that is your time to negotiate. The same is true for the question 'Will your career break affect your future working arrangements?' If you have taken a career break to have a baby or raise a child this question may be used to find out about your child-care arrangements. Again, it's important to present a positive picture and assure the recruiter that all necessary provisions have been made and that your work patterns will not be affected. Remember the time to negotiate is after you've been offered the job.

Your questions
Is there anything you would like to ask me/us at this stage?

All properly conducted interviews should give you a chance to ask questions at the end. If no opportunity is given and you do have questions, ask at the end of the interview when would be a convenient time to raise them.

At this stage don't feel you must ask questions if you have none. A simple 'no questions at the moment thank you, we seem to have covered the main points' will suffice. If you are going to ask questions don't enquire about salary, vacation, bonuses or benefits. Your aim is to show how you can benefit the company by what you have to offer. The time for meeting your own requirements is at the negotiation stage. If really pressed for an answer on salary, indicate first that you are more interested in the opportunities the company has to offer and then name a salary range. This technique will leave you and the recruiter room for negotiation without causing embarrassment.

Finally

1   Make sure you don't criticise your previous employer however much you feel like doing so! This really should be avoided as much as possible. The interview should be kept positive at all times. If you *really* feel you must be negative about your employer, then prepare how you do it and ensure you show how *you* have made the best of a bad situation.

2   If you find you are arguing with the recruiter, make your points firmly and politely and leave yourself room to back out of a confrontation, so that you can both save face. The aim is to be assertive *not* aggressive.

3   At the end of the interview it is possible that you won't have had the opportunity to give the recruiter a vital piece of information about yourself, which could help you win the job. If this is the case, include this information when you are given your chance to ask questions.

4   If you know you are waffling or answering a question badly, have the confidence to stop. State that you're not answering well, and go back to the beginning. The recruiter will respect you for taking this course of action and you

won't miss out in answering what could be an important question.

The same technique holds for technical questions. If you can't answer say you don't know but that you would consult such and such a textbook to find the answer. The recruiter will move on to another question which you should find you can answer.

5   If at any time you don't understand the recruiter's question ask them to clarify; you don't want to answer the wrong question at the wrong time!

End the interview on a positive note. Thank the interviewer(s) for their time, shake hands if appropriate and make sure you know the correct way out of the room. Candidates have lost the chance of a job offer by walking into a cupboard instead of out of the door!

Positive and negative factors evaluated by a recruiter

During the course of the interview the recruiter will be evaluating positive as well as negative factors about you. Listed here are the negative and positive factors frequently evaluated and the reason these are often instrumental in leading to the hiring or rejection of a candidate.

Negative factors

Factor	Response
Unsatisfactory personal appearance/ inappropriate dress.	Would not represent the company in a positive way; unprofessional in front of visitors and clients.
Boasting as opposed to selling yourself. Presenting unwanted reports and documents.	Big-headed, egocentric and unable to follow directions.
Late/unprepared for interview. Unable to find way out.	Would not be organised/dependable on the job.
Overaggressive/ defensive/arrogant/ sullen attitude/ swearing.	Would be 'difficult' to work with and would not get along with other employees.
Inability to express thoughts or questions clearly.	Unsatisfactory verbal skills, unable to think to express ideas coherently.
Lack of interest and enthusiasm, especially when considering future goals.	Passive, no initiative, no imagination, no clear purpose.

Evasiveness.	Unwilling to take personal responsibility, will make excuses and blame others for mistakes. May well be hiding something.
Talking about domestic situation.	Immature, indiscreet, will bring personal problems into the office.
Criticising/ condemning past or present employer.	The recruiter will feel you are being negative and that you will criticise their company if they give you the job.
Failure to look interviewer in the eye, weak handshake nervous behaviour.	Lack of confidence or hiding something.

Positive factors

Factor	*Response*
Being on time and knowing where to go. Having with you all necessary documentation.	Organised and professional.

Smiling, sitting comfortably, looking recruiter in the eye.	Relaxed and positive. Able to function well under pressure.
Making *occasional* joke or amusing remark.	Confident, not afraid to present lighter side of personality.
Giving clear information on the company and the position.	Candidate taken opportunity to research company, will be thorough if given the job.
Talking positively about yourself and your achievements.	Able to present candidature positively and confidently.
Making suggestions about how you would tackle the job if it were offered to you.	Ability to initiate and innovate, having undertaken research.
Giving examples of how you made a success of your last job.	Will bring same sucess to new company and job.
Not giving in under pressured questioning. Remaining assertive.	Clear, concise thinker, able to present ideas logically when under pressure.

Asking intelligent questions about the position without going over the points already covered during interview.	Good research of position, able to deal positively with situation.
Showing clear career direction within the company.	Well motivated and ambitious. Thoughtful.

Keep a copy of these positive interview factors with your application form or CV and read through them before you go into the interview room. You will then be fully prepared to give the most positive impression of your candidature.

If the interview has gone well, towards the end you may become aware of behaviour by the recruiter which suggests they intend to offer you the job. This behaviour could include:

Leaning forward

Longer eye contact

Discussion about holidays, pay, hours etc.

Questions about the practicalities of employment, for example asking when can you start

The recruiter looking more relaxed

If you detect any of this behaviour it should enhance your overall presentation and confidence level. It does not mean, however, that you have definitely got the job, so do not become blasé and lose what could be your new position. Remember, to achieve *interview success* you must work hard and concentrate on your interview from the moment you enter the company building until the time you leave.

After the interview

Reviewing your performance

It is important to review your performance after each interview. The Review Chart will help you do this clearly and concisely. If the interview went well it will highlight the positive points you made, which you will want to remember and repeat next time. If the session was disappointing it will help you identify the areas and questions where you felt least confident. Once you have identified these you can build on the experience and ensure your performance is improved for subsequent interviews.

The Review Chart will also provide you with the detail you need if you are going to write a follow-up letter.

Review chart

Date of interview:
Company:
Interviewed by:
Title(s):

1 What I did well

2 Important successes/achievements I highlighted including my unique selling point

3 Good answers I gave

4 Poor answers I gave

5 Areas of questioning where I felt
   uncomfortable and unprepared

6 Things I will do differently next time

7 Any other points about this interview
   (positive and negative) which are
   important and which will be helpful for
   subsequent interviews

Try to complete a review chart after each interview. The sooner you can do this the better you
will remember the answers you gave. Given
time you can remember in a different light, or
even forget completely the uncomfortable
moments or poor answers you gave in an interview! Yet these are the very points that need to
be remembered and improved on for next time.

Follow-up action
If you are interested in the job it will benefit your application if you write a brief follow-up letter the next day. This should thank the interviewer(s) for their time and reaffirm your interest in the job. This letter will be added to the information the interviewer(s) already have on you and so will enhance the positive impression you have created.

Sample letter

Your name
Your address

Your telephone no.
(day and evening)   Date

The interviewer and company name
address

Dear Mr, Ms, Miss —
  First paragraph   Thank the recruiter for the interview in respect of the position of
. . . . Also include any reference numbers from the original advertisement.
  Second paragraph   Reaffirm your interest in the job. *Briefly* cover your reasons for wanting to work at this company. Also

mention any skills or experience that you might have overlooked during the interview.

Third paragraph Indicate once more that you appreciate being considered as an applicant and are available for interview if other managers wish to see you.

Yours sincerely,

YOUR SIGNATURE
(Your name printed)

If you are not successful after an interview you *must* build on the experience for future interviews.

1   Investigate (by contacting the company recruiter and from your own review) why you didn't get the job and formulate plans to improve your performance next time.

2   If you would still like to work for the company and the interview you had was positive, you could consider writing a holding letter. This thanks the recruiter for the interview and tells them you are still interested in their company and would like your name to be kept on file. If they felt you were a good candidate they may well call you back for interview if a similar vacancy arises. Remember, while job hunting it pays to be *politely persistent*.

The following is an example of the type of holding letter you could write.

Your name

Your address

Date

The company's name and address

Dear (named person)

Thank you for your recent letter advising me that I have not been selected for the post of . . . . reference . . . . . at my recent interview.

I understand that you were looking for someone with more . . . . experience and hope that you were able to make an appointment for the post.

I wish you to know that I am still very interested in working for . . . . At my interview we discussed my background in . . . ./training as . . . . and I wonder if you are anticipating any vacancies in this area/these areas/at your . . . . branch. If so, I should very much like to be considered.

Would it be possible for you to retain my CV or could you let me know when you will next be advertising?

With many thanks for your advice in

this matter and for seeing me at the recent
interview.

I look forward to hearing from you in the
near future.

Yours sincerely,

YOUR SIGNATURE
(Your name printed).

Assessing the job offer

If you are selected by the company to fill the
vacancy, you will receive an offer of employment. Use the following checklist to help you
decide whether to accept the job. The job
search is a two-way process and you must
ensure you are going to be happy in the new
job and are satisfied with the conditions of
employment before accepting the company's
offer. If the job is not right for you and you
accept it, you will soon begin to feel disillusioned and depressed. This can affect your
confidence level and result in poor job performance, which will be unacceptable to you
and your new employer. So think very carefully before accepting a job offer, especially if
it is the first one you are offered after a period
away from paid work. You may be tempted to
take any job to get back into full-time employment, but many job searchers say that taking
the first job that 'came along' was a mistake

and resulted in a further job-searching exercise which left them feeling demoralised. Remember, if you have been successful at interview once you will be again, and the right job may well come from a subsequent interview.

Job offer – checklist

Put an asterix (*) by your three most important needs.
Award points out of 10 for the following:

Needs	Points
Salary	—
Benefits	—
Prospects for training and promotion	—
Interesting work	—
Friendly environment	—
Convenient location and suitable hours	—

Results

46+   This job, as presented to you, meets your needs and looks promising. Before you accept the position make sure the company's terms and conditions of employment match your expectations.

30–46   The job is of some interest to you. Is it possible to talk to the company's personnel representative and renegotiate those aspects which you gave low marks? This is particularly important if they are the categories marked *. How long will you have to accept the aspects of the job that don't satisfy you? If it is only for a relatively short time then it may be worth accepting the job for the longer-term rewards and experience it will give you.

Below 30   It does not appear that this job meets your own needs. Do you have all the necessary and correct information about the job? If you have, it may be best to refuse the job offer and use the experience as a good indication of how to achieve interview success to secure the right job.

When assessing the offer, concentrate particularly on the areas you might want to develop for the future. A job might hold your interest for six months to a year while you are still in the learning phase but what are the prospects for you after that? If you are an executive secretary or administrator, will the company offer you training prospects on new office equipment, or the opportunity to progress into a full management position once you have proved yourself in your first job? The complaint most often voiced by job seekers is that a job was 'sold' to them as having more responsibility than was actually the case. So beware of titles such as 'Company Administrations Executive', 'Executive Personnel Co-ordinator' and the like – they may well be masking glorified clerical positions, when your aim has been to make a first or second management move.

The same is true if you are entering a profession with a recognised training programme, for example nursing, the law or banking. Will the institution you train with promote you once you are qualified or will you have to move location on completion of your training? This is particularly important if you are a late entrant into a profession, with domestic or financial ties which prevent you from moving around the country in order to further your career.

In each instance the procedure remains the same: before you accept the offer investigate all aspects of the company and the job as fully as you possibly can. No recruiter will mind you asking questions at this stage because they are keen for you to fill their vacancy. If there is something that you're not happy about then now is also the time to negotiate. A company is unlikely to offer you a further £5000 (unless you have exceptional skills!) but if you are incurring additional expenses it might be prepared to offer £500–£1000 or promise you an early salary review date.

So, if you are unhappy with an aspect of a job offer and as long as you are prepared to compromise, it is worth negotiating with a prospective employer to enhance the terms of employment offered to you. But do try to be flexible. If you make too many demands you may end up losing the offer altogether, so think very carefully before contacting the company and make sure you leave yourself and the recruiter room to manoeuvre. If the company meets your request then you can accept the offer knowing you have positively helped your position. If the company won't meet your demand (or agree a compromise with you) at least you will have tried and can now assess whether to take the job as originally offered.

5 Speculative approaches and the hidden job market

In addition to applying formally for jobs, through advertisements in magazines, newspapers and through recruitment agencies, it is important to expand your network of contacts and seek informal help from every quarter. You should let not only your friends and relatives but also your work contacts and past acquaintances know you are job searching, and ask them to talk to people on your behalf. If you are hoping to gain promotion within your present company then you must also make sure your managers, and the managers of the department you wish to join, know who you are and what you can do.

If you have had a career break or are redundant (and can bear the thought of working for the same company as your partner!) then ask your partner to talk to his or her colleagues and contacts about you. Talking things through in this way may well lead to avenues of opportunity that you had not considered.

The following statistics apply whether you are looking for in-company promotion or a job with a new company.

Performance at interview or in your present job counts for 10 per cent of your job search. Another 30 per cent is based on the *image* you project, either at work, if you are looking for a new job within your present company, or at your interview when dealing with a potential new employer. That leaves 60%, and that 60% is based on *exposure*. How well known are you? Have you seen round a new company and talked to its managers about their new product or pay scheme? Have you attended their open day and spoken to as many people as possible? Wherever you are job searching the rule remains the same: *the better known you are the better chance you have of securing the job you want.*

Speculative approaches

Making yourself known to companies is also important when considering potential vacancies. Many vacant jobs are never advertised. They are filled by someone, like yourself, writing a speculative letter or making a telephone call to a company to see whether it has a suitable opening. The most positive result of this is that sometimes an employer creates a vacancy for the right candidate, so that you could find yourself being interviewed alone without competition, before a vacancy arises or a job is advertised. Even if the company doesn't go as far as to create a vacancy for you it may well interview you for a post it has already advertised, or interview you ahead of the field for a job it had anticipated advertising. Remember, if you get a job in this way you will already have saved your new company the cost of advertising and recruiting! The advantage of making speculative approaches is that it demonstrates your initiative to an employer, who in turn is likely to be impressed that you want to know more about the company and employment opportunities within it. The disadvantage is that you may well find yourself writing a great number of letters, thus drawing considerably on your own time and resources. You must be careful to achieve the right balance between a realistically researched approach and a speculative waste of time. For example, don't write to a company that has recently conducted a successful local recruitment drive or one that has recently announced falling profits. Instead you should begin by writing to companies you think will be most likely to have openings for someone with your qualifications and experience. Find out from public libraries or the company itself the name of an individual to write to. The *Kompass Directory*, kept by your public library, is another excellent source of company information which also gives geographical locations.

Keep your letters short, typed if possible,

and to the point. The example letters from Chapter 3 will help you.

Telephone contact

If you have said in your letter that you will phone the company in six days time to arrange a meeting you must do just that. If you didn't say you would phone but haven't heard from the company after ten days then you should phone by way of a gentle reminder!

Before phoning make sure you know what you are going to say. Write down in advance the points you wish to make and practise speaking out loud. If you are on your own this is particularly important. Few things sound stranger than hearing your own voice on the phone if you haven't spoken all day!

The company recruiter you speak to is probably busy with other work and while you are geared up to talk about yourself they may not know who you are or what you want. Introduce yourself clearly and slowly, telling the recruiter why you are phoning and then leaving them space to talk. Listen carefully to what they say and have a pen and paper with you to write down any instructions they give you. Repeat back dates, addresses and times of appointments to make sure you have them right. It pays to be politely persistent; if they can't see you, ask them if there is someone else you can speak to or information they can send you. Try not to take no for an answer, but don't be rude or aggressive and never swear even if your frustration has reached boiling point! Stand up rather than sit when talking on the phone; this will help you maintain a *positive* frame of mind.

If the firm will not see you, it is simply because they do not have the time. *Do not* take it as a personal reflection on you. They may, however, keep your CV and contact you when a suitable vacancy arises, so you have lost nothing by making the approach.

The speculative meeting

If the company does see you the ball is firmly in your court. There are three possible outcomes:

1 You may be told that while there are no vacancies at present your CV will be retained by the company and you should apply formally when they next advertise.

2 There are a number of openings shortly to be advertised and the company will see you for a formal interview.

3 They will interview you for an unadvertised vacancy as soon as possible.

The rule of a speculative 'information meeting' of this kind is to ensure that you and your potential employer do not lose face over the situation.

It is essential, therefore, that you take control at the outset showing interest, an enquiring attitude, listening and being forthcoming when invited. Treat the discussion as an exploratory first interview. Remember, you may be invited back for a formal interview and should leave a good impression which you can build on next time.

Find out all you can about the company before you meet the person who interviews you. The more informed interest you can show the more likely you are to be considered for future vacancies.

The interviewer will ask you questions about your skills and experience based on your CV, so ensure you prepare for these thoroughly and don't forget to read chapter 4 of this book before you meet your prospective employer!

Developing the speculative approach

Make sure the interviewer understands why you want the meeting. You cannot ask directly for a job, but by asking questions about the firm's future development and vacancies within the industry in general you will demonstrate that you are seriously job searching.

The interviewer will be impressed by your interest in the company. During the discussion you should ask if there is anyone else in the company you could talk to, for example in a specific named department. This will not only show further evidence of your interest but will also give you another contact. When you come to the end of your discussion thank the interviewer for their time and ask the only direct question of the meeting:

'Would you be interested in keeping my CV?' If you have created the right impression this request is unlikely to be rejected. Indeed it could well result in your CV being passed on to another interested party.

Outcome

The interviewer may well feel they have met someone they regard as a potential employee for the company.

For your part:

1 You will be considered for future vacancies with the company.

2 You should have come away with another contact.

3 You will have learnt a great deal about the organisation and administration of the firm which will stand you in good stead for future interviews.

4 You will know when and where vacancies are likely to be advertised.

5 You can be reasonably confident that your CV, once retained, will be passed around to relevant departments.

By taking control of the discussion and showing interest, you will have enhanced your
reputation without asking the million-dollar
question, 'Can you offer me a job?', which can
cause embarrassment on both sides.

As soon as possible after the meeting, it is
sensible to write a letter of thanks to the person you have seen. The letter should
summarise the points you discussed and con-
firm any action plans. Again, use the examples
from chapter 3 to help you.

Writing this letter is confirmation of the
points you should have raised at your discussion:

1   a declared interest in the company

2   another name to add to your list of
    contacts

Make sure you keep all your options open and
don't hesitate to write to other companies and
pursue further contacts with them. A second
interviewer, for example, may well refer you
to a manager in a sister company or someone
else within the industry. In this way you will
develop your *networking* process, all the time
building your knowledge of the industry as a
whole, your range of contacts and, above all,
the growing possibility of *finding the right job*.

The approach

While the speculative approach can often achieve the best results, it is also the one which can prove the most disappointing.

Often you will find the manager you have contacted cannot see you. Even if you are given the chance of a meeting, it is unlikely to result in an immediate job offer. The best way to prepare for these eventualities is to be realistic.

The approach is geared to increasing your knowledge and extending your list of contacts. It will take some time, perhaps weeks or months, before your contacts will present you with a firm job offer or formal interview, so be prepared for several preliminary discussions at which you must always provide the interest and enthusiasm.

Never go to one of these meetings expecting to be offered a job; the chances are you won't be. Unfulfilled expectation can only lead to increased frustration and disappointment. Secondly, don't be too 'pushy'. Treat the meeting as an exchange of information; if you over-emphasise your wish to be offered a job you may cause embarrassment and may lose a potentially helpful contact. If treated correctly, however, you will find your contact network both useful and ultimately rewarding.

6 Your new job

Starting a new job is an exciting and challenging prospect but in the first few weeks it can also be quite overwhelming. You will want to make the transition period as stress-free as possible, especially if you have been away from paid work for some time, or have been with your previous employer for many years.

What can you expect? Will your colleagues, staff and managers be helpful and encouraging and will you be able to cope with the office routines and technology? The answer to these questions is *yes*, providing you do your homework and take your time. If you expect miracles on day one you will end up being disappointed!

Before day one

Find out as much as you can about the company before you start your new job. If possible visit your new office and have lunch with your prospective colleagues. If you are taking on a management role you may find your senior managers are already arranging this for you. The more you know about the company and its working practices on your first day the less of a newcomer you will appear. This, in turn, will increase your confidence level.

You must use your initiative and be prepared to work hard to be accepted. If, for example, you find the office word-processing or computer system is different from the one you are used to, ask to be put on a familiarisation course as soon as possible. There's always a great deal to be learnt at the beginning of a new job and the more homework you do beforehand the quicker you will settle in. Your aim is to become an established member of staff as quickly as possible, so make sure you attend as many company induction programmes and meet as many people as you can, right at the start.

Day one and beyond

The following 12-point checklist will help you through your first weeks in your new job. We don't suggest you pin it on your wall (!) but it is a good idea to keep it with you as a gentle reminder of the best way to approach your new position.

Your new job 12-point checklist

1 Be on time!

Being late in your first weeks, even by a few minutes, creates a poor and irresponsible impression of you in the minds of other employees.

2 Always carry a *personal notebook*, or diary, and a pen with you.

As you are introduced, write down the names of your new colleagues, members of staff and other employees/ departments with whom you will be working. In addition make notes about important departmental information and policies. As you add new information this will become an invaluable reference book for you. *Don't lose it!*

3 Don't assume you can use your colleagues and manager's first names.

You may have worked for an informal organisation where most employees used each others' first names. The same may not be true of your new company and you should always ask people how they prefer to be addressed. This is also true for people who have 'nicknames'. They may not mind being called by such names by those they've known for years but it may not endear you to them in your first weeks.

If you are a manager coming from a formal organisation where you were called Mr —, Miss —, Mrs —, Ms —, or 'Sir' or 'Madam' and your new company uses first names, you will need to get used to this as soon as possible. *Don't* make yourself unnecessarily unpopular early on, by insisting on your new staff and colleagues adopting working practices from your old company.

4   Measure up the office atmosphere before making changes.

During your first few days, take mental notes regarding the way people act and dress, unwritten office procedures (such as who makes the coffee and the length of lunch breaks) and the general atmosphere in your new office/ department. If there's a procedure you don't like, make sure you know why it's done and how others feel about it, before you try and change it.

5 Always ask questions when something is unclear – as you are being trained, write key learning points in your personal notebook or diary.

There is no shame in asking for the demonstration of a procedure or added clarification of policy instructions. Any questions you leave unanswered in the initial stages may turn into mistakes when you are on your own. As a manager your staff will respect you for asking them and your colleagues and managers will be willing to help you in your first weeks.

6 For small problems have your manager, colleagues or established member of staff suggest a specific person to help you.

Remember, once you've met them, write their name, job title and phone extension in your book for future reference.

7 Never complain about your job to your staff or colleagues.

Complaining is never a good policy – you never know who might overhear you and *literally* take you up on a chance remark; 'I'm sick of this place', 'I'm leaving' . . . 'I hate so-and-so', etc. Complaining is especially ill-advised when you're new; you will immediately be judged as a person who looks for faults in jobs and people and you will give yourself a bad reputation.

8 Avoid discontented colleagues' complaints and gossip.

Change a negative conversation into a positive one by asking for advice on departmental policy. Listening to someone else's complaints/ gossip will heighten your own awareness of minor or imagined issues. It is essential for you to remain positive!

9 What to do if you are handed several assignments at once.

Immediately ask for the deadline of each assignment, then prioritise from there. If you are in the middle of an assignment for one manager and another gives you an 'urgent' assignment, ask the first manager if theirs can wait. If *not*, have the managers work it out between themselves; it is their problem, not yours.

10 Learn about overall organisational activities.

If you understand how your job links to others and how your department fits into the company's overall structure, you will not only work more intelligently, but will also find you become valued for your understanding. People who know only their own responsibilities and nothing else – go nowhere.

11   Realise that every job has some duties that are boring.

Just accept them. Once you become established, you can discuss them with your manager and senior colleagues and determine whether or not they are rightfully your responsibility.

12   Don't rush to decorate your work area.

You could alienate yourself by sticking up your favourite posters and surrounding your desk with executive toys or teddy bears! Observe how others in the company, at your level, organise their desk and surrounding area and, at least initially, curb your more outrageous tendencies!

Above all, be receptive. Listen to what other people have to say and take time to learn the duties and intricacies of your job and department before making changes. This is especially true if you are a new manager. Staff resent a new person coming in and changing their established routines from day one.

Take time to listen to their opinions and make changes slowly and surely, consulting your staff each time you introduce a new procedure or change an existing one. In this way you will establish a good working relationship which will make the transition period that much smoother for all concerned. Remember, *the sooner you get to know the people, the job and the surroundings the more rewarding your new job will be.*

What if it doesn't work out?

All new jobs bring with them bad experiences. You may not find you have the responsibility you hoped for or you might have a particularly difficult manager or member of staff to deal with. Whatever the problem, give it quiet consideration and above all *time*, to pass over. What looks like a major problem in week one may become negligible by the end of month one, when you will have established allies amongst your staff and colleagues who can help you over the rough patches.

If after a few months there are still major problems you should go and talk them over with personnel, your manager or the head of your department. Normally a talk of this kind will clear the air and adjustments will be made in your working practices. If you get no results from this, however, and you still feel unsatisfied and frustrated you will have to think of leaving. There are two rules to follow in this situation.

1 Try and wait at least nine months before moving jobs again or you may have trouble explaining to a prospective employer why you only stayed a short time. This is especially important if you have no long periods of employment recorded on your CV. You don't want to get a reputation for being a difficult employee or a drifter.

2 However much short-term satisfaction it may give you don't resign on the spot and storm out of the office! You probably need your salary and you should look for work from a position of strength, i.e. with the security of a job behind you. It will help you and creates a much better impression for potential employers. The message is clear: *even if you hate the job and the company sit tight until you find a new one.*

You will have to put the event down to experience and evaluate what you will do differently next time. Ask yourself whether you rushed into the first job you were offered without thinking through what was really on offer? Were you misled by the recruiter at the time of the interview and promised responsibility that never came to light and did you do your *homework* on the company before taking the position offered? Whatever the reason for your disappointment, build on your experience so that the next job you take is the *right job* for you.

7 Useful references and additional reading

The following are available from your local public library.

Reference books

1 *Kompass Register of British Industry and Commerce*
This lists information on over 28,000 companies, most with over 50 employees. It is particularly useful for identifying companies in a given geographical location.
Publisher: Kompass (published annually)

2 *The Times 1000*
An annual review of the top 1000 UK companies.
Publisher: Times Books (published annually)

3 *Yearbook of Recruitment and Employment Services*
Lists recruitment agencies by job, job category and geographical area.
Publisher: Longman (published annually)

4 *Centre for Professional Employment Counselling Recruitment Guide*
A comprehensive directory of recruitment agencies and search consultants in the United Kingdom.
Publisher: CEPEC (published annually)

5 *Telephone Yellow Pages*
Useful for classified local searches.

6 *Floodlight*
Information on London-based day and evening classes. Courses include creative writing, self-presentation, interpersonal skills and assertiveness.
Publisher: Association of London Authorities and London Borough Associations (published annually)
To find out about regional classes across the UK, contact your local education authority.

General reading

Career change
*What Colour is your Parachute? A Practical
Manual for Job Hunters and Career
Changers.* Richard Bolles.
Publisher: Ten Speed Press (1989) distributed
in the UK by Airlift Book Company

An A–Z of Careers and Jobs. Diane Burston.
Publisher: Kogan Page (1988)

Managing Your Own Career. David Francis.
Publisher: Fontana (1985)

Career Change: new working directions.
Leslie Morphy.
Publisher: Hobsons (1987)

Interviews
The Interview Game. Celia Roberts.
Publisher: BBC Books (1985)

Self-employment
*Going Freelance: self employment with
minimum capital.* Godfrey Golzen.
Publisher: Kogan Page (1989)

Starting a Business on a Shoestring. Michael
Syrett and Chris Dunn.
Publisher: Penguin Books (1988)

Assertiveness
Be Assertive. Beverly Hare.
Publisher: McDonald Optima (1988)

Assertiveness at Work: a practical guide to handling awkward situations. Ken and Kate Back.
Publisher: McGraw Hill (1982)

Effective Speaking. Christina Stuart.
Publisher: Pan (1988)

Government and other departments

> Department of Employment
> Tothill Street
> London
> SW1H 9NF

Their information branch HQ can advise you if you have any queries about your entitlement to redundancy payment and supply you with leaflets on benefit.

> Central Office of the DSS
> PO Box 21
> Stanmore
> Middx
> HA7 1AY

General information leaflets on benefits, including family credit.

Training Commission –
Central Information Unit
Moorfoot
Sheffield
Information on secondment opportunities and
retraining.

Citizens Advice Bureau
(See telephone directory for your local branch)
Advice on all financial, housing, redundancy
and legal matters.

2x

Lansdowne Recritment (LTD)
Park House 207
TItE Vale London W37QP

Desch J Mills
Enterprise

The Hermitage

45 chuch sket
EPScon Sirrey,

McStphn ALFRon
Construction Ctel
Hooten South Wirral
L66 7WD

Matthew Hall
Engineering Lim

Chris Bennett
employment manager
that
101-108 Tottehom
M-   Cout RD
              London W1 A 1BT

Overseas recruitment
services

35 Golden Square
London W1
   439 9481

Tarvis The Sons
PLE 289
Vauxhall Bridge RD
London SW1V 1T1t

DO

TECHNICAL

071

...w) LTD

31-33 College road

Harrow Middlesex

HA1 1BA (071
inner london

071 863 0884 / 088
081

Taylor Woodrow Grap
345
Ruislip Road
Southall Middlesex
UB1 2QX

Mr U Hart ~~Construction~~
Company personnel service
manager

SHEPHERD Construction Ltd
Blue Bridge Lane York YO1 4